Watford
A pictorial history 1922-1972

Below: View of Watford High Street from the air in 1922

Alan W. Ball B.A., F.L.A.
BOROUGH LIBRARIAN

Watford

A pictorial history
1922-1972

PUBLISHED BY
WATFORD BOROUGH COUNCIL
1972

The Borough Arms

In the top third of the shield are the Arms of St. Albans to commemorate the long association between that city and Watford. The "harts" represent the Herts in Hertfordshire.

In the lower part of the shield occur two escallop shells taken from the Arms of the Earl of Clarendon, Charter Mayor. The wavy blue and white lines represent the ford in Watford.

The fasces in the centre denote magisterial authority.

The motto "*Audentior*" is a quotation from Virgil's *Aeneid* VI, 95: "tu ne cede malis, sed contra *audentior* ito, quam tua te Fortuna sinet". (Yield not thou to ills, but go forth to face them *more boldly* than thy Fortune shall allow thee.)

ISBN 0 903408 00 7 (Cloth)
ISBN 0 903408 01 5 (Paperback)

Printed in Great Britain by Sun Printers Ltd. London and Watford

URBAN DISTRICT OF
WATFORD

Notice is hereby Given, That the Undersigned,

THOMAS REGINALD COLQUHOUN DILL

BARRISTER-AT-LAW,

the Commissioner appointed for the purpose by the Lords of His Majesty's Privy Council,
will hold an

INQUIRY

AT THE

Council Chamber, 14, High Street, Watford

IN THE COUNTY OF HERTFORD, ON

FRIDAY, the 10th day of MARCH, 1922

At 10.30 o'clock in the Forenoon, into the subject matter of the **Petition of
Certain Inhabitant Householders of the Urban District of
Watford, Praying for the Grant of a**

CHARTER OF INCORPORATION

in accordance with the provisions of the Municipal Corporations Act, 1882,
and into any matters incidental thereto.

All Householders, Owners and other Persons, having an interest in the matter of this
Inquiry, who may desire to be heard before the Commissioner, may attend and they
will be heard.

Dated this 1st day of March, 1922.

T. R. COLQUHOUN DILL

**9, OLD SQUARE, LINCOLN'S INN,
LONDON, W.C. 2.**

C. H. PEACOCK, LTD., PRINTERS, WATFORD.

Above: Commissioner's Inquiry into the proposed Charter of Incorporation. March 10th, 1922

General Introduction

This work has been produced to mark Watford's Golden Jubilee as a Borough and is a contribution to the extensive and lively programme of Jubilee events, which is making 1972 such a memorable year in the town's history.

In the 1920s Watford, like the rest of the country, was only slowly recovering from the death and destruction of the First World War. Remembrance Days brought out huge crowds of people and among them must have been few who had not lost a close relative. The phrase about a 'Land fit for heroes to live in' had already turned sour and produced the counter jibe of needing to be a hero before you could live in such a land.

However in 1922, Watford forgot current problems to celebrate its elevation to Borough status. From 1850 to 1894 there had been a Local Board of Health, still commemorated by Local Board Road, off the Lower High Street. From 1894 to 1922 this had been replaced by an Urban District Council and finally in 1922 came the Charter of Incorporation with a considerable rise in status and the office of Mayor. The programme of celebrations for Charter Day on October 18th still exists cataloguing a lively series of events. The Charter was handed to the first Mayor, the Earl of Clarendon, on the Borough boundary at the junction of Haydon Road and the London Road by the then M.P. for the district, Mr. Dennis Herbert. Afterwards there was a procession through the town, still miraculously preserved on an early, jerky newsreel, showing lorries decked out with

Above top: Mr. Dennis Herbert, M.P. for Watford, hands over the Charter to the town's first Mayor, the Earl of Clarendon, on the Borough boundary at the junction of Haydon Road and London Road

Above: The Earl of Clarendon is on the right

6

flags and banners bearing such stirring slogans as the one sported by the London & North Western Railway, 'We lead—trade follows'.

Fifty years ago, Watford already had a population of 46,000, but in many ways continued to resemble an overgrown country town. A noisy market was still held in the High Street where the bleating of sheep, the squealing of pigs and the lowing of cattle were more in evidence than the new-fangled products of Messrs. Nuffield & Ford. Cassiobury House was yet to be torn down and the Cassiobury estate built, while work was almost completed on the first large-scale council house project of the Harebreaks estate. The Watford by-pass had not been constructed, the Central Library was still in Queens Road and the Town Hall offices in Upton House, in the High Street. The development of North Watford was only really beginning with Odhams Factory, the Meriden multi-storey flats and the M1 undreamt of wonders for the future.

The pages that follow tell the story of Watford's fifty years as a Borough. They are designed to be complementary to the two other more general pictorial histories of the town. The first of these was produced by Mr. R. C. Sayell, F.L.A., my predecessor in office as Borough Librarian, for the Borough Festival of Britain Committee in 1951, and the second by Mr. J. B. Nunn and the Watford Camera Club to mark the Club's Diamond Jubilee in 1963. Inevitably, however, there is some overlapping, but my main hope is that many people still resident in the town will, by browsing through these pages, recall sights familiar over many years, which will bring past memories vividly alive once again.

Charter Day, October 18th, 1922

Wet weather had no dampening effect on the spirits of the townspeople of Watford, who obviously enjoyed their great day and made the most of the handing over of the Charter and the subsequent procession up the High Street.

Below: Part of the subsequent procession up the High Street. The fire brigade team in the front were from Sedgwick's Brewery

Top left: Two forms of motive power, the old . . .
Centre left: . . . the new . . .
Below left: . . . and the merely frivolous

Right: Civic before ecclesiastical dignity. The Town Clerk, Mr. William Hudson, holds an umbrella to shield the Earl of Clarendon while the Bishop of St. Albans, the Right Rev. Michael Furse, comes a poor third

Above: The Proclamation of the Charter being read from the Essex Arms Hotel in the High Street. The Hotel used to be situated almost opposite the entrance to Market Street

Right: Memories of the trenches

9

Local Government and the Town Hall

Most people take very much for granted the services provided by local government and probably only think about them when it comes to paying the rates. However, if a comparison is made between the present time and 1850, when the Local Board of Health was first set up in Watford, it is instructive to see what an enormous difference sound local government has made to the whole environment. In 1850 sewerage, drainage and a pure water supply were almost non-existent and road paving and lighting in their infancy. Because of these conditions, public health hazards were enormous and modern amenities like libraries,

Left: The Town Hall was completed in 1939 and stands at the main crossroads in the centre of the town. It is a simple, dignified and functional building. The architect was C. Cowles-Voysey

parks and swimming baths beyond the wildest imagination. The changes that have been brought about over the intervening years have been the result of patient and often humdrum work by elected representatives and local authority chief officers and employees. Often there has been far more criticism than praise of those who have tried to serve their fellow citizens, but although the ruthless operation of a dictatorship may achieve more spectacular results, the steady progress of local government in Britain has achieved far more in the long run for its people and has done so without the odious and sinister methods of a totalitarian regime.

Below: The entrance to the two assembly halls which are part of the Town Hall. The main assembly hall seats 1,600 and is in constant use for concerts, dances, and a wide range of social functions. It has especially good acoustics and the main gramophone record companies use it regularly for recording purposes

11

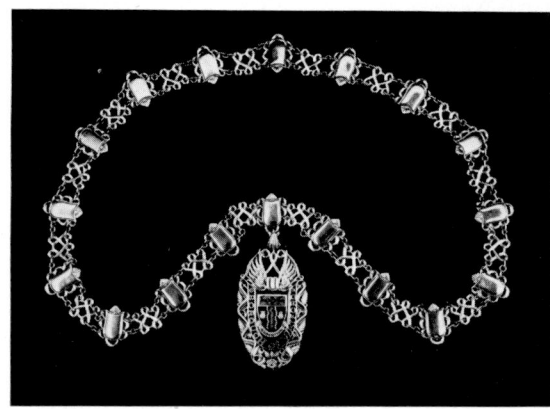

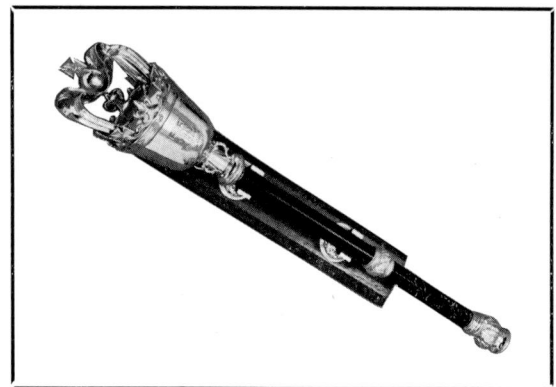

Civic Regalia

Above top: The Council Chamber in the Town Hall

Above left: The Chain of Office of the Mayor of Watford

Left: The town's Mace. A symbol of regal and civic authority which is carried before the Mayor at ceremonies and is present at Council Meetings

12

They shall grow not old, as we that are left grow old:
LAURENCE BINYON — *For the Fallen*

Above: The two minutes' silence actually in progress in 1924 outside the Council Offices at Upton House. At the centre of the crowd stand the Mayor, Alderman Ralph Thorpe, and the Town Clerk, Mr. William Hudson. The cinema posters are in marked contrast to the solemnity of the occasion

Right: Poster for Remembrance Day Civic Observance of Two Minutes' Silence 1924

BOROUGH OF WATFORD

REMEMBRANCE DAY

It is earnestly requested
that the

Two Minutes' Silence

will be observed in Watford
at 11 a.m. on REMEMBRANCE DAY,

TUESDAY, NOVEMBER 11th
1924

The Mayor, Aldermen and Councillors will attend outside the Municipal Offices, High Street, at 10.50 o'clock on TUESDAY MORNING, to take part in the TWO MINUTES' SILENCE.

R. A. THORPE,
MAYOR.

Watford Printers Limited, 58 Vicarage Road, Watford.

West Herts Post

No.22899 Established 1887   THURSDAY May 13th 1926   Price ONE PENNY.
SPECIAL EMERGENCY EDITION.

THE STRIKE: TO-DAY'S NEWS: LOCAL POSITION.

Thursday afternoon.

Although the General Strike was "called off" yesterday, the Strike still operates in Watford, but the position may change at any moment.

Apparently, the Council of the Trades Union Congress, or the Headquarters of the various Unions, have left a good deal of authority in the hands of local Strike Committees, or those Committees have taken it. According to our information, the Central Strike Committee in Watford are adopting this policy:- That they will not permit their men to return to work until the proprietors of all the works affected have given undertakings that all the men on strike will be re-instated in their old positions.   At one big employment centre, at any rate, that guarantee is not forthcoming; the National Omnibus Company have declined to give it; and the Strike Committee take the line that they will not permit their men in any trade to go back until that question is settled. One striker, apparently speaking the view of the Central Committee says "We went out in a body, and we are going back in a body".

On enquiry at the Garage this morning, we were informed that the only action being taken is that "men are being engaged on a temporary basis" and that "the question of re-instatement of strikers is under consideration in London.

The National gave notice a day or two after the Strike commenced that the men would be paid on the following Friday, on handing in their uniforms, at the Depot. This, they refused to do. The Company next issued a letter to each man that he had broken his agreement and that unless he reported for work by 9 a.m. yesterday (Wednesday) his place would be filled.   Manned by volunteers, about six buses left the Garage yesterday, To-day about 15 buses are out.

As regards railwaymen, we are told that every man who signs on will be re-instated on the consent of the Chief General Superintendent. All men who wish to be re-instated have to sign on before to-morrow, Friday May 14th. The Company will put men to work as their services are deemed necessary in each department.

LOCAL FATALITIES.

As a party of Londoners, in a motor car were passing through Abbots Langley, on Sunday evening, the driver, Harry Bassett, in attempting to avoid a motor cyclist, ran the car up an embankment, with the result that the car was overturned and the six occupants were seriously injured. One of them, Elizabeth Carter, aged 16, 13 Wigmore-street, London, died on Monday at Watford Hospital. The inquest, which opened yesterday, was adjourned.

At Watford Hospital this morning, a verdict of "Accidental death" was returned in the case of James Harries (57) 32 Leavesden-road, who died on Tuesday. He was run over by a dispatch rider motor-cyclist at Garston on Tuesday morning.

Mr. Harry Kent having resigned, Mr. F. Pagnam has been appointed Manager of Watford Football Club. Slade, Smith (F.) Foster, Swan & Morris have re-signed. Terms have also been offered to Prior, Stephenson & Strain. The following players are "open to transfer":- McCullock, Eggleton, Papworth, Harris and Smith (E.) Free transfers have been given to Williams, Fryer, Gregory, Hewitt, Baker, Mummery, Carter, Wright, Rance and Bell.

The Old English Fair, arranged for Whitsun, on behalf of Watford Hospital, has been postposed until August Bank Holiday.

The "West Herts Post" will appear in its usual form as soon as circumstances permit. Our mechanical staff is still "out".

The General Strike

Because of the bad state of the coal industry, the government in 1925 granted the coal-owners a year's subsidy and set up a commission of inquiry. Although the commission recommended a re-organisation of the industry in March 1926, the subsidy was allowed to expire in May of that year and the coal-owners said that they could only employ miners on lower wages than were currently being paid.

A national strike was called by the T.U.C. as from midnight on the 3rd May in support of the miners and this lasted until 13th May. In Watford, as in the rest of the country, crowds gathered by day and volunteers kept a certain number of essential services running. The effect on labour relationships was traumatic and in combination with the depression that followed in the 1930s, over-shadowed the lives of many ordinary people in the inter-war years.

Left: The General Strike emergency edition of the West Herts Post for May 13th, 1926

Above: People reading a news bulletin outside Trewins
Below: A crowd gathered at the junction of the High Street and Market Street. A bus has just passed up the High Street

16

Cassiobury

Sir Richard Morrison acquired the property of Cassiobury in 1545 and soon afterwards commissioned the building of a house, which was completed after his death by his son Sir Charles, and about which very little is known. When his great grand-daughter Elizabeth married Arthur, 1st Lord Capel of Hadham, the whole estate came to the Capel family. Arthur was executed in 1649 for his loyalty to Charles I, but at the Restoration Cassiobury was given back to his son, who was created Earl of Essex, and who commissioned Hugh May to rebuild the house. In 1800 the 5th Earl of Essex engaged James Wyatt, who remodelled the house in the fashionable Gothic style. During the Edwardian period some of the grounds were sold for building development and in 1922 Cassiobury House was itself disposed of and finally demolished in 1927. At the time of the sale it contained many fine works of art, which are now scattered throughout the world. A particularly pleasing staircase, thought to be the work of either Grinling Gibbons or Edward Pierce, is in the Metropolitan Museum of Art in New York, while some of the materials salvaged at the time of the demolition have been built here and there into houses in the town.

Several of the cottages on the edge of the estate survived for many years after the House, the three most notable being the Shepherd's Lodge at the corner of Shepherd's Road and the Rickmansworth Road, the Swiss Cottage and the Lodge Gates into the Park from the centre of the town on the Rickmansworth Road. The cottage called Cassiobridge Lodge remains virtually unchanged to this day at the juction of Gade Avenue and the Rickmansworth Road, while

Left: Cassiobury House from the air in 1922

Below: The Inner Courtyard of Cassiobury House

Above: One of a series of stained glass roundels depicting the Labours of the Months, formerly in Cassiobury House and now at the Victoria and Albert Museum

part of the stable block was reconstructed to form the very attractive old people's home called Cassiobury Court in Richmond Drive.

For many of the older people in the town, Cassiobury House brings back affectionate memories and great sadness that such a noteworthy building has not survived to the present day. It is, however, to the eternal credit of the Urban District Council, and after 1922 the Borough Council, that often against the fiercest opposition, large areas of the grounds of the House were retained to form in Cassiobury Park one of the finest areas of open space close to a town centre anywhere in the country.

Below: The East Front of Cassiobury House

Left: The Main Staircase of Cassiobury House by either Grinling Gibbons or Edward Pierce. This is now in the Metropolitan Museum of Art in New York

Above: The Library in Cassiobury House in its heyday . . .

Right: . . . and stripped prior to demolition

19

Left: The Pond was one of the features of the grounds of Cassiobury House

Below: The Stables of Cassiobury House were reconstructed to form the present old people's home in Richmond Drive called Cassiobury Court

Right: A superbly carved wooden surround, which once framed a picture from the rich collection in Cassiobury House, is shown here in conjunction with the final demolition notice, as a melancholy reminder of the passing of an important country seat

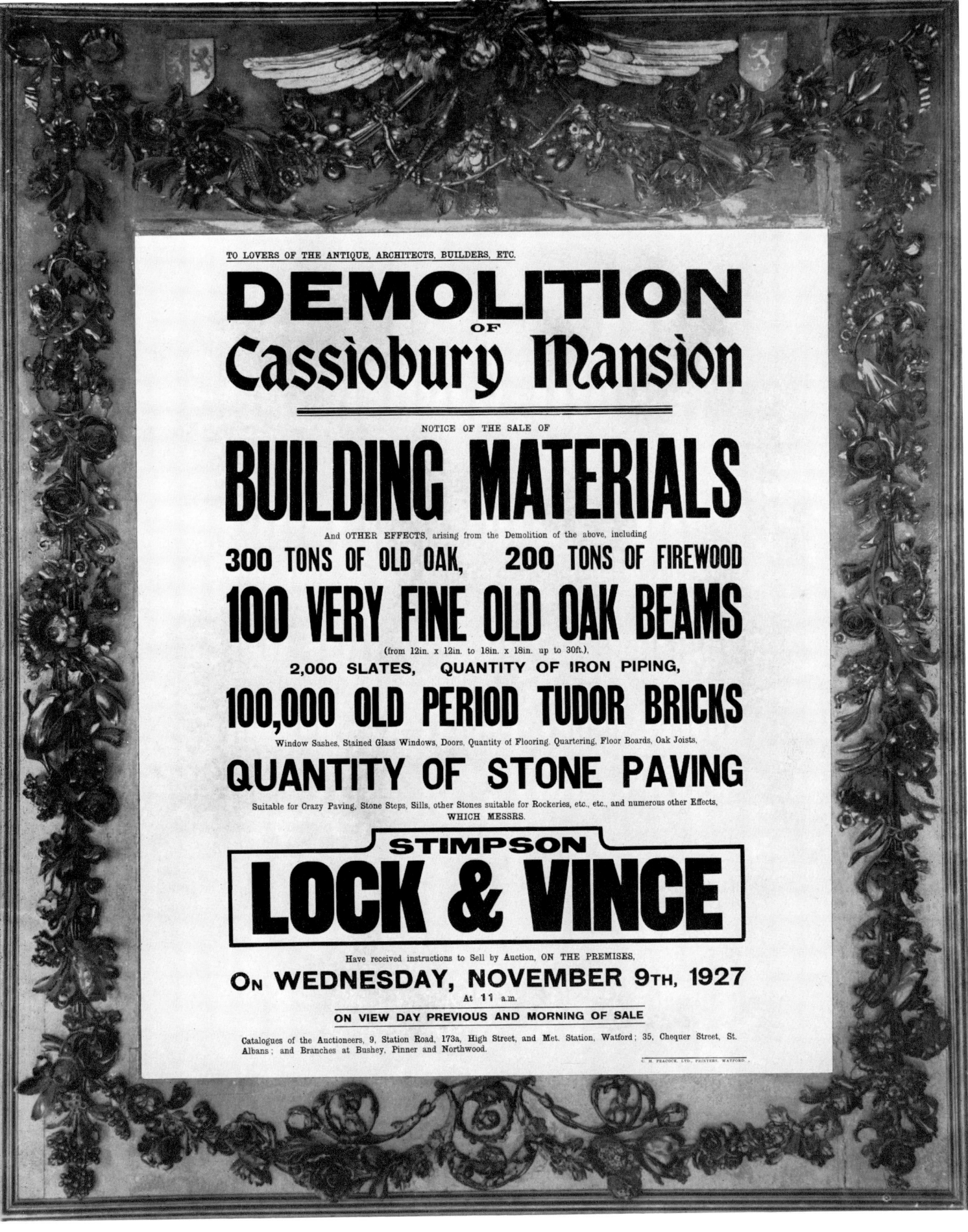

TO LOVERS OF THE ANTIQUE, ARCHITECTS, BUILDERS, ETC.

DEMOLITION
OF
Cassiobury Mansion

NOTICE OF THE SALE OF

BUILDING MATERIALS

And OTHER EFFECTS, arising from the Demolition of the above, including

300 TONS OF OLD OAK,   200 TONS OF FIREWOOD

100 VERY FINE OLD OAK BEAMS

(from 12in. x 12in. to 18in. x 18in. up to 30ft.),

2,000 SLATES,   QUANTITY OF IRON PIPING,

100,000 OLD PERIOD TUDOR BRICKS

Window Sashes, Stained Glass Windows, Doors, Quantity of Flooring. Quartering, Floor Boards, Oak Joists,

QUANTITY OF STONE PAVING

Suitable for Crazy Paving, Stone Steps, Sills, other Stones suitable for Rockeries, etc., etc., and numerous other Effects,
WHICH MESSRS.

STIMPSON
LOCK & VINCE

Have received instructions to Sell by Auction, ON THE PREMISES,

On WEDNESDAY, NOVEMBER 9th, 1927

At 11 a.m.

ON VIEW DAY PREVIOUS AND MORNING OF SALE

Catalogues of the Auctioneers, 9, Station Road, 173a, High Street, and Met. Station, Watford; 35, Chequer Street, St. Albans; and Branches at Bushey, Pinner and Northwood.

C. H. PEACOCK, LTD., PRINTERS, WATFORD

Left: The Mill in the grounds of Cassiobury House, which survived until 1956

Above: The Lodge Gates at the entrance to Cassiobury Park near the town centre were a much-loved feature of Watford. They were demolished for the Central Area Redevelopment Scheme in 1970

Above: James Wyatt had a brother called Samuel, who helped him in many of his commissions. Samuel often worked with a proprietary brand of stucco called Higgins' Cement and when the Lodge Gates were demolished in 1970, the crests on them were found to be of stucco and not stone, as had long been imagined. A brick bearing the initials S.W. was also discovered built into the structure

Below: The brick shown was removed from the Lodge Gates on demolition, the initials C.H. standing for Cassiobury House. It is clear from an early sketch that the Gates were built in two sections, that on the right when entering the Park from the town centre being the older. This brick came from the older section

Left: The Swiss Cottage. This stood in the grounds of Cassiobury House and was used for picnics and open-air entertainments. It survived until the Second World War when it was burnt out, probably by somebody sleeping rough

The Grove

Below: The Grove was the home of the Earls of Clarendon from 1753 to 1935. The house was built by Sir Robert Taylor in 1756, enlarged by Matthew Brettingham in 1780 and had further extensive alterations in 1850. Unlike Cassiobury House, it still survives and is used by the British Railways Board as a Productivity Services Training Centre. This view is of the South Front of the building

THE ESSEX ALMSHOUSES, CHURCH ROW, WATFORD.
(Reproduced by kind permission of the proprietors of the "Watford Observer")

These eight cottages, so well known to residents in the town, were built in 1580 by Francis Russell, second Earl of Bedford, for the use of eight poor women from Watford, Kings Langley or Chenies. They have been in continuous occupation ever since.

No provision was made in the Trust for the upkeep of the buildings. They have been maintained hitherto from private sources which are no longer available.

The Churchyard without these old buildings will no longer be recognisable as the centre of old Watford. With some modern structure in their place the harmony of the whole Churchyard will be destroyed.

His Worship the Mayor is appealing for funds to repair the buildings and save them from demolition. About £650 of the £800 required for complete restoration has been collected or promised.

Sympathisers who desire to aid in raising the remaining £150 are earnestly requested to enter a contribution overleaf.

(Issued by the Watford Amenities Preservation Society.)

THE ESSEX ALMSHOUSES.

SAVE THE OLD PEOPLE'S HOMES
—— AND ——
OUR ANCIENT BUILDINGS

MAYOR'S FUND

FLAG DAY, 2nd JULY, 1932

Above and right: The poster and appeal sheet are examples of the material used in the 1931/32 campaign

Below: An exterior view of the Almshouses during restoration in 1959. The original doorways are now windows and the main access is now at the rear of the Almshouses

The Bedford or Essex Almshouses

The Bedford or Essex Almshouses were built in 1580 by Francis Russell, Earl of Bedford, 'that eight poor women . . . might inhabit and be maintained in the said almshouses'. Three hundred and fifty years later they had fallen into decay and were in grave danger of being demolished. However, Alderman William Bickerton, who was Mayor during the municipal year 1931/32 was the moving spirit in a campaign for their preservation and restoration. Thus an early and enlightened piece of conservation has ensured that these charming cottages survive in the heart of Watford and their humble character makes a pleasing contrast with the nearby Parish Church of St. Mary, the Free School and the Multi-storey Car Park.

Left: An interior view of one of the rooms in the Almshouses also taken during restoration in 1959

Below: A view of the Almshouses taken in 1972

NOBLE LOCAL EFFORT: To Honour the Dead, To Relieve Suffering.

£46,000 NOW ASSURED, BUT £14,000 MORE REQUIRED.

WATFORD & DISTRICT PEACE MEMORIAL HOSPITAL
Rickmansworth Road

Above: An example of appeal literature for the Peace Memorial Hospital of December 1922

Hospitals

The return of peace after the First World War saw the construction by public subscription of the Peace Memorial Hospital which was opened in 1925 by H.R.H. The Princess Royal and later extended. The other principal hospital in the town is Shrodells which has grown out of former workhouse accommo-dation. These two groups of buildings are now known together as the Watford General Hospital and the Shrodells site is being rapidly developed on modern lines. Already there is a new maternity unit, a new psychiatric unit and a postgraduate medical centre.

Below: The Official Opening of the Peace Memorial Hospital in June 1925 by H.R.H. The Princess Royal. The Princess is seen here leaving the building

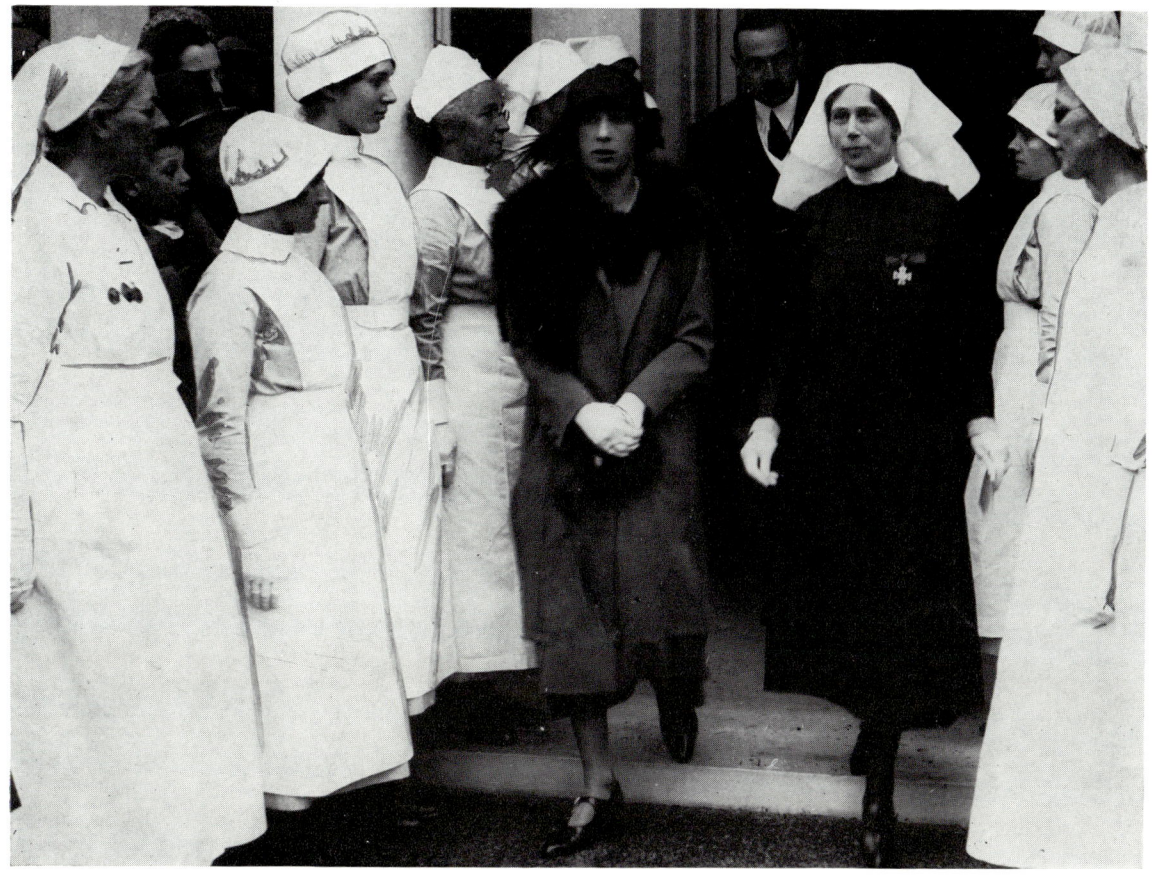

27

PHOTO BY BOLTON, P... WATFORD PORTR...

Above left: The exterior of the Peace Memorial Hospital in the 1950s with the War Memorial in front. The latter now stands outside the Town Hall opposite the Central Library, as its original site was required for road works in connection with the Central Area Redevelopment Scheme. The figures on the War Memorial were the work of the well-known local sculptress, Mrs. Mary Bromet

Left: Exterior of the new Maternity Unit at Shrodells

Above: A ward in the Peace Memorial Hospital in the 1920s

Right: A ward in the new Shrodells Maternity Unit

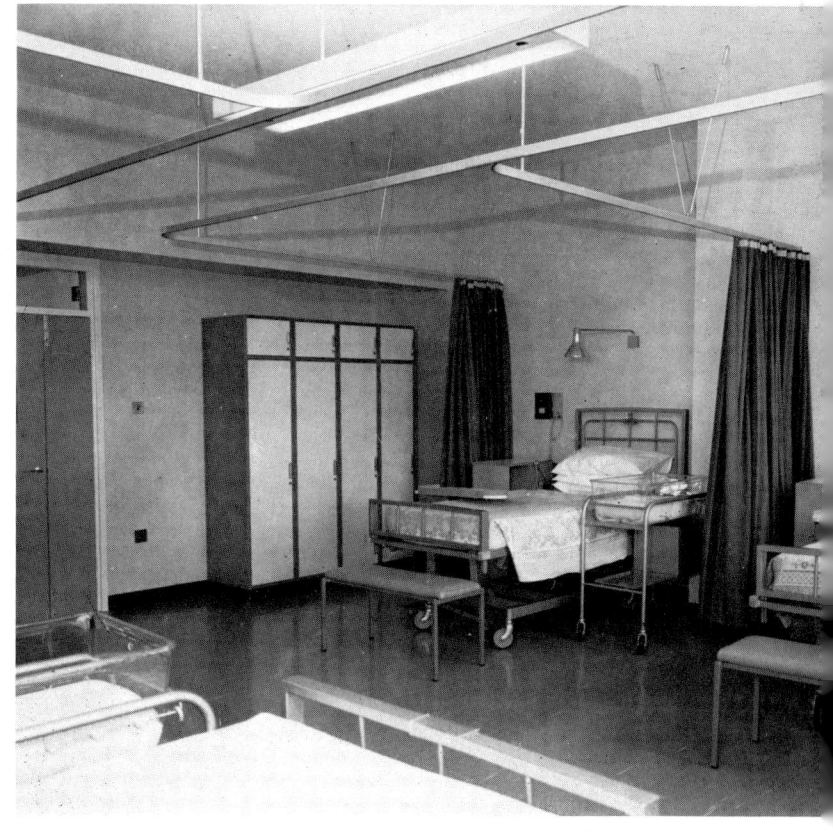

Floods

Some of the houses and business premises in the Lower High Street were built with steps up to their entrances to guard against flooding from the nearby River Colne. In 1928 and especially 1947 when the snows melted after an arctic Spring, the Lower High Street was inundated, while in 1936 a cloudburst brought similar conditions in the centre of the High Street.

Right: July 1936. In the High Street near the junction with Clarendon Road

Below right: March 1947. A tricky piece of footwork

Left: January 1928. All aboard with Dobbin

Below: January 1928. It is not clear whether some form of tow is being offered by the milkman, but the more primitive form of transport seems to be winning hands down in these conditions

Above: March 1947. Literally the end of the road   *Above top:* March 1947. Put your best oar forward

Posters and Announcements

One of the most interesting ways of recalling the past is to look at a selection of posters and announcements for events and happenings now long since faded into obscurity, but which at the time were possibly burning issues of the day. Typography, like everything else, has its fashions and the very way that letters appear on a public announcement often tells you whether this was a rush job or something produced at leisure with the backing of a great deal of thought and effort.

Below Left: Mr. William Newman was the Borough Engineer at that period
Below: The official ending of the Middle Ages. 'Decollation' means 'beheading'
Bottom Left: It is not clear whether the sentiments of the last line are an encouragement or discouragement to would-be intrepid aviators
Bottom right: The price quoted is an eloquent reminder of how times have changed

---

BOROUGH OF WATFORD

Coal Emergency Directions, 1926

COAL PERMITS

NOTICE

No coal or coke for domestic consumption may be supplied or acquired without permit from the Borough Fuel Overseer.

The quantity allowed is 2 cwts. of coal and 4 cwts. of coke per fortnight, or alternatively, but not in addition, 28 lbs. of coal and 28 lbs. of coke per week may be purchased over the counter without permit.

Neither coal nor coke may be supplied or acquired if the stock on the premises exceeds 5 cwts. of coal or 10 cwts. of coke.

Permits may be obtained on and from Friday, 5th November, 1926, on application at the Coal Office, Upton Road, between the hours of 9.30 a.m. to 1.0 p.m. and 2.30 p.m. to 5.0 p.m., or through the post if a stamped addressed envelope is enclosed.

W. W. NEWMAN,
Borough Fuel Overseer.

Municipal Offices,
WATFORD,
3rd November, 1926.

THE FAIRS ACT, 1871
(34 & 35 Vict. cap. 12)

WATFORD FAIRS

The Secretary of State for the Home Department hereby gives notice that by Memorial dated 2nd June, 1927, a representation has been duly made to him by the Watford Town Council that Fairs have been annually held at Watford on the morrow of Trinity Sunday and the two days following, and on the day and morrow of the Decollation of Saint John the Baptist respectively, and that it would be for the convenience and advantage of the Public that the said Fairs should be abolished. On the 15th day of July, 1927, the Secretary of State will take such representation into consideration, and any person who may desire to object to the abolition of the Fairs, should intimate his objections to the Secretary of State before that day.

Home Office,
Whitehall.
8th June, 1927

FLYING!

The World-Famed Berkshire Aviation Tours beg to announce

PASSENGER FLIGHTS

From **5/-** Each

AT TOLPITS LANE

Near, Watford West Railway Station,
WATFORD,

From AUGUST 21st to SEPTEMBER 2nd
INCLUSIVE.

Daring Exhibition of Crazy Flying
On SUNDAY at 4.15 and 7.45 p.m.

The Exhibition consists of Looping, Spinning, Rolling, and all the things that can be done on an Aeroplane by Experienced Pilots.

The B.A.T. has carried over 80,000 people safely, visited over 500 different towns, flown for six years (winter and summer), and in every town visited are known for their Safety First methods, and the pleasure given to their passengers. No stunting is given to ordinary passengers; if you do want a few we can do them, but it will cost you a little more. The oldest passenger carried was Mrs. Ann Sissons, at the age of 103 (a world's record), and the youngest 3 years. We will carry anybody from 103 to 3, and everyone will enjoy the experience.

FLYING DAILY from 10 a.m. to DARK
3-SEATER MACHINES IN USE ALL THE TIME.
All Flights done on B.P. the British Petrol.

Admission to Field 6d.   Children 3d.

WATFORD ! You will be under the earth one day. Get off it !

King & Hutchings, Ltd., Printers, Uxbridge.

BUCKS EXPRESS

Watford
- TO -
Oxford Circus

2s. Return

Commencing this Thursday
September 26th

COACHES START FROM BUCKS GARAGE
HIGH STREET.

½ **Hourly Service from 7.30 a.m.**

Luxurious
Comfortable Coaches

BOROUGH OF WATFORD

Town Clerk's Office,
Watford.

24th January, 1936

Dear Sir ~~or Madam~~,

Death of H.M. King George V

I am desired by the Mayor (Mr. Councillor Last) to invite you (~~your representatives~~) to be so good as to accompany him to Divine Service at the Parish Church of St. Mary on Tuesday the 28th January at 3 p.m.

The Mayor hopes you (~~your representatives~~) will be in attendance at the Municipal Offices not later than 2.30 p.m.

Robes will be worn.

Kindly fill in the attached form and *let me have it by return of post.*

Yours faithfully,

William Hudson

Town Clerk.

P.S. A Special Meeting of the Town Council is summoned for 2 p.m. to pass loyal resolutions and the procession will form up at the close of the Council Meeting.

E.   R.

Proclamation

of

His Majesty KING EDWARD VIII

at Watford

FRIDAY, 24th JANUARY, 1936

His Worship the Mayor (Mr. Councillor E. C. Last, J.P., M.P.S.), being charged with the Proclamation of HIS MAJESTY KING EDWARD VIII in the Borough of Watford will attend at the Municipal Offices, Watford, on Friday, 24th January, 1936, at 12.30 p.m., and will then and there proclaim the King.

W. HUDSON,

Town Clerk.

MUNICIPAL OFFICES, WATFORD
22nd January, 1936.

PRINTED BY WATFORD PRINTERS LIMITED, 34 VICARAGE ROAD, WATFORD.

Reprinted from " Mother & Child," March 1938

WELFARE CENTRES

DAY NURSERIES

SOCIAL SERVICE WORKERS

ORPHANAGES

INSTITUTIONS and HOSPITALS for young children

HOP-PICKING and FRUIT-PICKING ORGANISATIONS

ETC., ETC.

PLEASE NOTE

THE "JUST-SO" SAFETY HARNESS

(British,   Reg. Trade Mark)

For Infants & Toddlers

(Registered Design No. 774263)

Keeps a baby safe everywhere, all the time, whether in cot, pram or chair. This safety device, of bleached or unbleached webbing, is washable and adjustable. It is suitable for infants of six months and upwards. The Toddler's outfit includes a leading rein.

The Harness is not available through the usual trade channels and is obtainable only from

**The Distributor
THE "JUST-SO" HARNESS SUPPLY
212, Hagden Lane, Watford, Herts.**

who will forward full particulars and terms on application.

SAMPLE OUTFIT, comprising Harness No. I (for Infants) and Harness No. 2 (for Toddlers), in bleached webbing, together with packet of pram fittings, may be had post-free for 2s. 9d.

THE " JUST-SO " SAFETY HARNESS has the approval of the Mothercraft Training Society and other eminent authorities on infant-rearing.

NOTICE

BREAD RATIONING

(Borough of Watford)

EXTRA COUPONS
FOR ADOLESCENTS

(11-18 years)

Distributed from the Small
TOWN HALL

From **9** a.m. to **5** p.m. (Saturday excepted)

MONDAY JULY 8th

to

FRIDAY JULY 19th
1946

**IDENTITY CARDS
AND NEW RATION BOOKS MUST BE PRESENTED**

RE-PRINTED BY WATFORD PRINTERS LIMITED, 34 VICARAGE ROAD, WATFORD, HERTS.

Above top: The King is dead . . .

Above: An example of Watford enterprise

Above top: . . . Long live the King

Above: Even after the end of the Second World War many problems remained

Cinemas and the Palace Theatre

In these technologically advanced days the early, jerky years of the cinema now seem very far away. Many of these motion picture houses were designed like dream palaces and had varying styles of lavish decoration. For a brief hour or two the harsh world of the 1920s and 1930s could be shut out by Hollywood epics, although newsreels brought a new style of pictorial journalism that made people only too aware of disturbing events on the Continent. The rise of television in the 1950s signalled the end of great days of the cinema and many have now closed or been turned into bingo halls and supermarkets. Perhaps what marks the end of an era most significantly is a current move to preserve one or two cinemas as important examples of the architecture of the inter-war period.

Although the Palace Theatre had been a regular feature in the life of Watford over many years, it was only in 1965 that it became a civic venture. In that year the Borough Council set up the Watford Civic Theatre Trust in consultation with the Arts Council of Great Britain. There is now a professional company presenting repertory with a wide range of productions including many contemporary plays. Amateur societies also perform in the Theatre and so does the Theatre for Youth, a forward-looking venture started in 1967 to encourage young people to become interested in the drama.

Below: The Central Hall Cinema in King Street. It is now a bingo hall

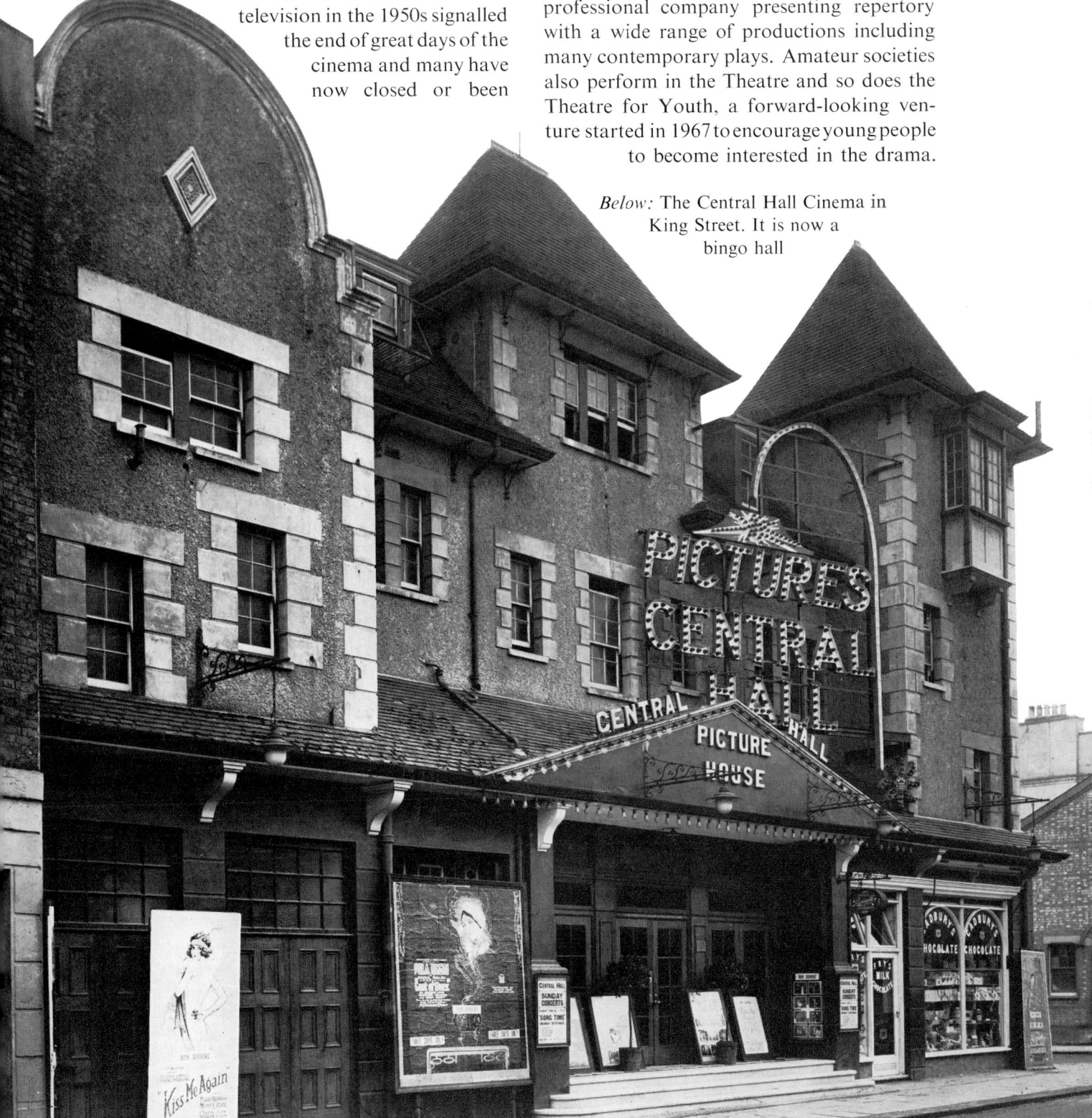

Above: The Plaza was afterwards renamed the Odeon. It is now Caters Supermarket and the Top Rank Centre. The present Odeon is farther down the High Street and was formerly the Gaumont

Below: Centre spread of May 1929 programme entitled 'Forthcoming Attractions'

BEBE DANIELS.
Appearing in the Paramount
Picture:
" HOT NEWS."

Above: Also taken from the May 1929 programme

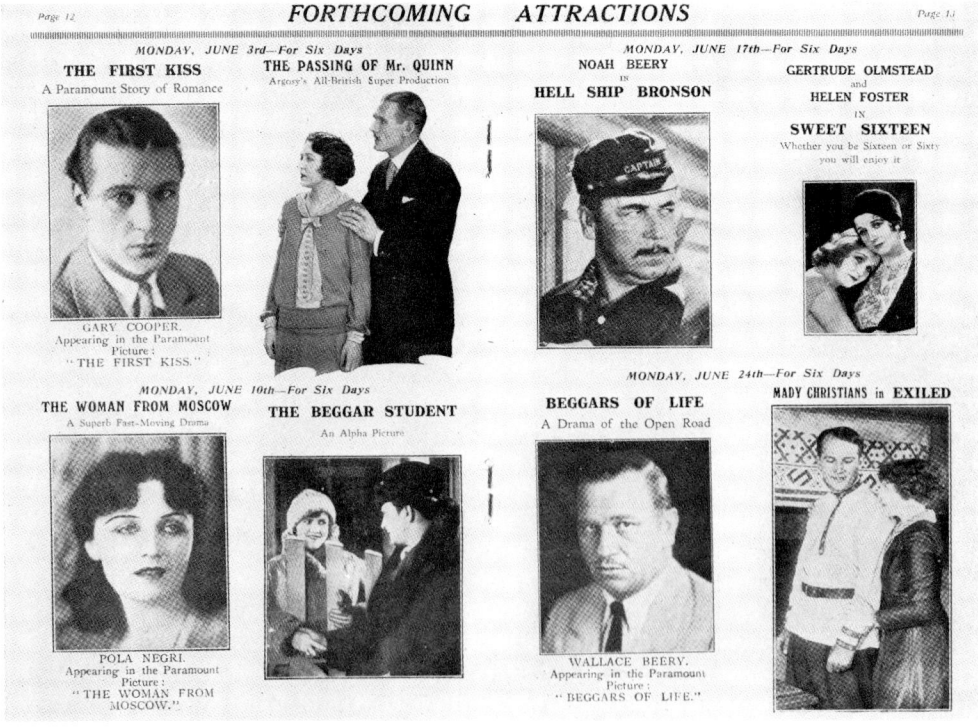

Below: The interior of the Palace Theatre. The view is of 1967 after re-decoration

Below bottom: A scene from the production of Shakespeare's *Julius Caesar* at the Palace Theatre in March 1971

The Second World War

From this distance in time the Second World War brings back a kaleidoscope of memories. Evacuees, looking small and lost, clutching an odd assortment of cases and boxes, taped-up shop windows, people huddling in damp Anderson shelters, finding that your train had overshot the platform because of the blackout, Dig for Victory, National Savings Drives, hearing the heavy drone of Dorniers and Heinkels and the frightening and peculiar whistling sound of a stick of bombs coming nearer and nearer. Also there were the dreaded telegrams and letters of condolence telling of the death in action of a loved one or that a doodlebug had flattened the home of a friend. Even though Watford escaped lightly compared with other parts of the country, there were numerous air-raids in which people were killed, the worst being on the night of Saturday July 31st, 1944, when a flying bomb landed on houses in Sandringham Road and St. Albans Road and there were nearly forty deaths.

Above left: Personnel under instruction, November 1938

Left: The ARP Recruiting Office, October 1938

Above top: Firemen prepared to operate under a gas attack

Right: At the outbreak of war, children were often evacuated comparatively short distances away from major cities and many of them had to be moved to other localities when bombing started in earnest. These children are from Essendine School, which is in Maida Vale. Note the house prices on the advertisement hoarding behind these evacuees leaving Watford Junction Station

Above: White lines being painted on a lamp post at the corner of Upton Road to help both pedestrians and motorists see it in the black-out

Above: A shop window taped-up against possible bomb-blast

Below: Conscripts signing on at Watford Labour Exchange

Top right: The delivery of Anderson shelters

Bottom right: Two girls with their dolls' prams watching men dig trenches in Cassiobury Park

Above left: Air Cadets under instruction
Left: An early reverse. The news of the sinking
of HMS *Courageous* on 17th September, 1939
Above top: "Did you remember to lock the
back door?" . . . or gas masks for adults . . .
Above: . . . baby . . .
Right: . . . and even faithful Fido

The Train Crash at Harrow and Wealdstone Station

On October 8th, 1952, a local train was waiting peacefully in Harrow & Wealdstone Station when a Perth-London express hurtled into it, and scarcely had any further time elapsed before a London-Manchester express ploughed into the resulting wreckage. The following week the *Watford Observer* reported: "Curtains were drawn in many front windows this week, and funeral processions set out from the streets where a few days before laughing young men and girls had cried out 'Goodbye, Mum', before catching the fateful train." Thirty-seven of the 112 people killed came from the Watford area and the then Mayor, Alderman L. C. Johnson, visited all the bereaved relatives individually. He said afterwards: "One went to minister to them and came away feeling one had been ministered to. For courage and fortitude I have never seen the like."

Below: Journey's End

Transport

The line from London to Birmingham came through Watford in 1837 and since that date the town has always had a close connection with the railway and many railwaymen have lived here. A locomotive suburban depot was established in 1890 and St. Andrews became known as the Railwayman's Church with sleepers from the original London to Birmingham line built into one of the walls. One of the most exciting periods of development has come in the past ten years with the electrification of the line to Birmingham, Coventry, Manchester and Liverpool, and the consequent speeding up of running times. In 1925 the Metropolitan Railway came as far as Cassiobury Park Avenue, but a plan to push on to the High Street and use what is now the Grange G-Plan furniture shop as its terminus came to nothing. London Transport's green country and red central buses are a familiar sight in Watford's streets and the route 142 still exists, although the contemporary single-deck vehicles make a marked contrast to the double-deckers which trundled down the High Street in the 1920s.

Above: A panoramic view of Watford Junction showing a fast electric train on its way to Euston, with the goods yard in the background and the newly completed car park on the left

45

Above: The modern signal box at Watford Junction. At the front console sits Mr. Finlay Mackenzie, now retired from British Rail, who was formerly an Alderman of the Borough Council and Mayor in 1966/67

Below: A train of the type now on the fast service from Watford Junction to Euston, which runs every half hour

Above top: The *Royal Scot* passing through Watford Junction on August 26th, 1959. In these electrified times, the use of steam locomotives is confined to special journeys for railway enthusiasts

Above: The link between road and rail and air. A 727 Green Line Express coach, that provides a connection between Heathrow Airport and Watford Junction

47

Above: The opening of the Metropolitan Railway Station in Cassiobury Park Avenue in 1925. The railway is now part of the London Transport Underground system

Below: Metropolitan Railway buses dressed overall for a Shopping Week held from

October 20th-27th, 1928. The buses ran from the Metropolitan Station to the High Street

Below bottom: A Metropolitan Line train leaving Moor Park Station for Watford. The present rolling stock dates from 1962

Above: A 142 bus trundling down the High Street in the 1920s

Below: Nearly fifty years later the route number remains the same, but the appearance is somewhat altered

Above: A quiet corner in Oxhey Park by the River Colne

Below: Football practice in Garston Park

Parks and the Grand Union Canal

At one time a park was just an area of open space, which you took very much for granted. However, with the increasing pressures of urban life, more and more people now realise just how fortunate they are if they live within reasonable distance of one. In addition to Cassiobury, Garston, Meriden and Oxhey Parks and Whippendell Woods, Watford Corporation provides numerous playing fields and recreation grounds. Also, the town is indeed fortunate in having such a wonderful stretch of the Grand Union Canal within its boundaries. The section from Cassiobridge to Hunton Bridge is one of the most delightful of its whole length, and although little used for commerce is now attracting an increasing number of pleasure craft, especially at weekends. This gives life and movement in an agreeable and relaxed way, and allows people at locks and along the banks to appreciate just how pleasant it is to potter about in boats.

Above : Looking towards the bridge over the Grand Union Canal at the far end of Cassiobury Park. The rustic bridge crossing the River Gade is in the foreground

Below: Falling leaves in Cassiobury Park. This illustrates the tendency of boys' clothing to come apart at the middle when engaged in strenuous activity

Sport

Watford Rovers football club first played at the West Herts Ground in 1891, but in 1922 moved to the present Vicarage Road Ground and became Watford Football Club with its well-known nickname 'The Hornets'. The West Herts Ground is still used for cricket, hockey and tennis. Also Watford Corporation maintains a wide range of sporting facilities throughout the town. Archery, bowls, cricket, football, hockey, hurling, lacrosse, rugby and tennis are catered for in the numerous parks, recreation grounds and playing fields, while at Woodside, in addition to accommodation for many of the sports mentioned above, there is a running track of Olympic standards as well as an area for field events. Swimming is provided for at the Hempstead Road Baths and also at the new Leggatts Pool opened in 1972 for people in North Watford. This is a school pool that has been planned as a venture in dual use between Hertfordshire County Council and Watford Borough Council. The pattern of leisure activity is changing all the time and Watford now has a ski-slope for those people who wish to train for winter sports holidays. Golfers have the excellent West Herts Club course close to Whippendell Woods, which is one of the most scenic in the country.

Above left: Since 1961 there has been an active play leadership scheme during the summer holidays in Watford parks and recreation grounds. Here an impromptu game of rounders is in full swing

Left: The Grand Union Canal at the lock in Cassiobury Park. This view of 1955 shows cargo-carrying canal boats, which have now almost entirely given way to pleasure craft

Above: Two photographs showing tense moments at Watford Football Club matches on the Vicarage Road Ground during the 1971/72 season

Above: The ones who did not get in to the Vicarage Road Ground

Left: Children enjoying themselves in the Hempstead Road Baths

Below: Woodside Arena in the summer of 1965 with Cobb Green directly behind it

Right: A cyclo-cross race through the snowy glades of Whippendell Woods in February 1969

Below right: Learning how to put a correct tennis racquet forward

Above: The Central Library. A view taken in 1968

Below: "If I make myself very small, nobody will see me." A quiet corner of the mobile library

Public Library Service

The first public library in Watford was opened in 1874 at a building in Queens Road. In 1928 the present Central Library was constructed by the Borough Council and extended in 1961-63. The North Watford Branch Library was built in 1937 and a mobile service provided in 1957. In addition to the comprehensive book service for lending and reference to both adults and children, a record library was opened in 1969 and a new service for the elderly and house-bound is about to come into operation. One of the features of the past few years has been the series of exhibitions arranged in the Central Library exhibition hall. There are also facilities for meetings and lectures at both the Central and North Watford Libraries and these are heavily used throughout the year.

Above left: The village green atmosphere of a cricket match at Woodside

Left: The fascinating pattern of the Watford ski-run

Twin Towns

Watford has two twin towns, Mainz in Germany and Nanterre, a suburb of Paris. Although in the first instance contact was made at a civic level, these links have now been widened enormously and many sporting events have taken place, while parties of schoolchildren and students make regular trips to each other's towns, often staying with friends made on previous visits. There has also been a steady increase in the number of people from a particular trade, profession or industry travelling to see how their opposite numbers carry out their day-to-day work. All this activity has helped enormously to break down the barriers of dislike and suspicion that resulted from the Second World War, and with Britain's entry into the Common Market, it seems likely that an ever-increasing number of people will benefit from these links.

Left: Young visitors from Mainz being entertained in April 1958. Puffing contentedly on his pipe at the right is the then Mayor, Alderman Harry Horwood, who served for over forty years on the Borough Council until 1964 and was also County Councillor. In 1959 he was created an Honorary Freeman of the Borough and was awarded the O.B.E. in 1972

Below: The late Franz Stein, Oberbürgermeister of Mainz, receives a specially bound book at Odhams. There have been seven Honorary Freemen of Watford created since 1922 for outstanding services to the Borough. In order to mark Herr Stein's unrivalled contribution to the furtherance of the friendship link between Mainz and Watford, he was made in 1965 an Honorary Burgess or Citizen of the town, a new civic honour, which so far he alone has held. In this photograph taken in 1956, Herr Stein is in the centre, Alderman Edward Amey, Mayor in 1955/56, is on the left and Mr. Robert Kirk, at that time the Senior Executive at Odhams Watford Printing Works, is on the right

Above: A group of young people from Nanterre talking to Alderman Mrs. Mary Dodd, Mayor for 1971/72, in the Members' Room of the Town Hall
Below: A party from Nanterre being shown round the House of Commons. In the front row, the fourth from the right is M. Raymond Barbet, the Mayor of Nanterre. His wife, Mme. Barbet, is the sixth from the right, also in the front row. Next to her stands the late Councillor Leslie Wright, Mayor for 1965/66, with his wife. On the extreme left are Mr. Raphael Tuck, M.P. for Watford, and his wife. Behind Mrs. Wright is Alderman Edward Amey and behind Mme. Barbet, the late Alderman Reginald Gamble

Royal Visits

Royal visits are always a chance for a town to enjoy itself with people lining the streets to catch a glimpse of the distinguished visitors. In addition to the more formal ceremonies, there are always those heart-warming, informal moments, which happen quite spontaneously. Members of the British Royal Family are particularly skilled at giving these occasions a very happy air of dignity and charm. The two visits to Watford after the Second World War, which will stand out most in people's minds are those of H.R.H. the Duke of Edinburgh on 4th November, 1955 to open Woodside Sports Arena, and H.R.H. the Queen Mother on 3rd July, 1965 to inspect the 1st Battalion of the Bedfordshire & Hertfordshire Regiment (TA).

Below: H.R.H. the Duke of Edinburgh with the then Mayor, Alderman Edward Amey

Above: Part of the waiting crowd, some with
their official programmes

Below: H.R.H. the Duke of Edinburgh in a
relaxed mood with some children

61

Above: H.R.H. the Queen Mother being
greeted by the then Mayor, the late Councillor
Leslie Wright, on her arrival in Watford on
3rd July, 1965

Above right: H.R.H. the Queen Mother
talking to Mr. Ernest Baxter, O.B.E. He served
as a Borough Councillor for twenty years,
was Civil Defence Controller of Watford
during the Second World War and was
Chairman of Hertfordshire County Council

from 1958 to 1961. Mr. Harry Horwood stands
at the extreme right (see also the caption for
the upper photograph on page 58). Mr. Baxter
and Mr. Horwood are the two Honorary
Freemen of the Borough still living, of the
seven created since 1922. On the left of Mr.
Baxter is Alderman Edward Amey and on his
left again, the late Alderman Reginald Gamble
with Mrs. Gamble
Right: H.R.H. The Queen Mother shaking
hands with the Town Clerk, Mr. Gordon Hall

Freedom of Entry

On the 5th July, 1959, the 3rd East Anglian Regiment (16th/44th Foot) were granted the privilege, honour and distinction of marching through the streets of the Borough on all ceremonial occasions with colours flying, bands playing, drums beating and bayonets fixed.

Below left: The front page of the official souvenir programme

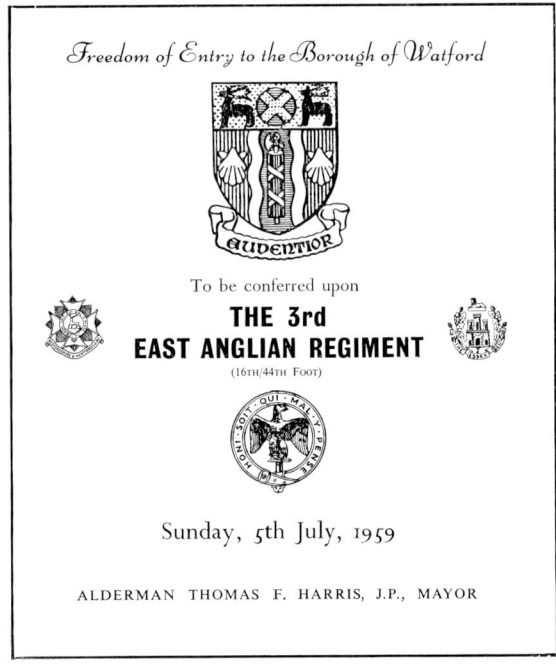

Freedom of Entry to the Borough of Watford

To be conferred upon

THE 3rd EAST ANGLIAN REGIMENT

(16TH/44TH FOOT)

Sunday, 5th July, 1959

ALDERMAN THOMAS F. HARRIS, J.P., MAYOR

Below: The band passing the saluting base outside the Norwich Union Insurance offices in the Rickmansworth Road

Bottom: The then Mayor, Alderman Thomas Harris, giving an address before handing over the official scroll conferring the Freedom of Entry to the Colonel of the Regiment, Lieutenant-General Sir Reginald Denning, K.B.E., C.B.

Education

The design of schools and colleges has undergone a revolution since the Second World War and the Boys' and Girls' Grammar Schools, that owe so much in style to the pioneering work of E. R. Robson and T. J. Bailey on buildings put up for the London School Board from 1871 until the early 1900s, are typical examples of early twentieth-century work. They contrast vividly with centres of higher education such as the Watford College of Technology, Cassio and George Stephenson Colleges, and buildings like Cassiobury Junior and Meriden Infants' Schools. The light, airy designs of contemporary schools and colleges are pleasant to look at and a stimulus to teachers, pupils, lecturers and students who work in them.

Above: H.R.H. the Duchess of Kent talking with a student in the Food Industries Department of Cassio College on 27th March, 1969, when she formally declared open the new building in Langley Road. Mr. Harold Elliott, the Principal of Cassio College, who retired in 1972, is to the left of the Duchess

Below left: The exterior of Cassio College

Below: The exterior of the College of Technology

Left: A student in the College of Technology doing practical work in film make-up for printing

Below: The exterior of George Stephenson College

Below bottom: The exterior of the Watford Boys' Grammar School

Right: A class at Meriden Infants' School

Right centre: The exterior of Cassiobury Junior School

Right bottom: A class at Cassiobury Junior School

Housing

The town has always been considered a pleasant place to live, situated as it is on the edge of delightful countryside. Before the First World War, the Nascot Wood area, West Watford and Callowland were developed, and in 1920 the Urban District Council created the first large municipal estate at the Harebreaks, which is now in process of being modernised. The inter-war years saw private development on the Cassio-bury, Tudor and Kingswood estates and since 1945 the Borough Council has pursued a vigorous housing policy. Large estates have been built at Garston Park, Holywell, Leavesden Green, Meriden and Woodside and also one at Hillside in Abbots Langley. The only two tower blocks constructed were at Meriden, so that housing has remained human in scale, and comfort and convenience have not been sacrificed for the sake of a spectacular skyline.

Left: Tower blocks on the Meriden estate
Below: Private housing on the leafy Cassiobury estate
Below bottom: Hollytree House is a block of Borough Council flats specially built for old people. The name was decided as the result of a competition among local schoolchildren

Right: Caractacus Green on the Holywell estate. The name comes from the Derby winner of 1863, which was owned by Mr. Charles Snewing of Holywell Farm
Below: A house on the Harebreaks estate with an enlarged downstairs window. This is being put in as part of the current modernisation of the estate
Below bottom: A modernised kitchen on the Harebreaks estate

Shopping and the Corporation Market

Watford is now one of the principal shopping centres of Southern England and in addition to a wide range of purely local businesses has an excellent selection of the national multiples. However, in the midst of these modern, streamlined enterprises, there is still a thriving market where a more individual approach is much in evidence and the sales technique of the costermonger lives on unimpeded.

Above top: Caters Supermarket beside the Pond. The Central Area Redevelopment Scheme has already altered this view

Above: The High Street Precinct

Right: A view towards Boots and the entrance to Market Street

70

Below: Pets Corner

Below bottom: All fingers and thumbs

Above: "I always say, it pays to try it on first"
Below: Not trading today

Commerce and Industry

The town is extremely fortunate in having a wide range of mainly light industries which has made it one of the most prosperous places in Britain. This background also helped to avoid in large measure the misery of the depression in the 1920s and 1930s when whole areas of the north of England were blighted. The list of products being manufactured includes aircraft engines, asbestos, plastics, chemicals, paints, pharmaceuticals, optical instruments, steel fabrications, electrical and electronic equipment, tools, jigs and mechanical handling devices, lorries, clothing and adhesives. Most outstanding of all is the largest concentration of printing in the world, with many of the supporting industries, such as paper making and printing ink manufacturing in the close neighbourhood. Clarendon Road, which was once lined with large and comfortable houses in spacious grounds, has since the Second World War been developed for office accommodation on a large scale.

Below left: The offices of Cape Universal Building Products Ltd. in Exchange Road. The architects are Douglas Stephen and Partners
Bottom left: Melton House and Star House, two office blocks in Clarendon Road
Right: The H. J. Heinz Building in Exchange Road. The architects are R. Seifert & Partners
Bottom right: The premises of S. Hille & Co. in St. Albans Road. The architect is Erno Goldfinger

Above: Odhams Printing Works in North Watford. The architect was Sir Owen Williams.

Above left: One of the many heavy duty vehicles that Scammell Lorries Ltd. produce in West Watford for use throughout the world.

Left: A section of the main press room at Sun Printers Ltd. showing print being delivered ready for packing from a 16 unit gravure machine.

Central Area Redevelopment

Nothing ever stands still and resistance to change is a deep-seated part of human nature, especially when it involves the alteration of places known over a long period of time. A comprehensive plan to redevelop the whole of the town centre was approved in 1968 after a public enquiry in 1965. This was the result of co-operation between Watford Borough Council, Hertfordshire County Council and the Central Government. At present, Phase 3 of this plan is well on the way to completion and its principal purpose has been to eliminate the notorious traffic congestion at the former Town Hall roundabout. To achieve this, it has been necessary to build four bridges, eight pedestrian subways and a large section of relief road. When the plan is completed, the north-western end of the High Street and the area between the Town Hall and Central Library will become traffic free precincts. The overall design of Phase 3 has been carried out by Mr. Richard Brand, the Borough Engineer and Surveyor, and his staff. The consulting engineers for the bridges and retaining walls are Ove Arup and Partners, while landscaping is the responsibility of A. G. Sheppard Fidler and Associates. The main contractors are Costain Civil Engineering Ltd. Many people find it very hard to visualise the tremendous amount of work involved and even more difficult to remember places that have disappeared entirely, but when construction is finished, Watford will have a new and exciting town centre.

Below: The new lighting columns seen against a slope of excavated soil are over 80 feet high

Below: The strain and tension of a crane driver doing a tricky job

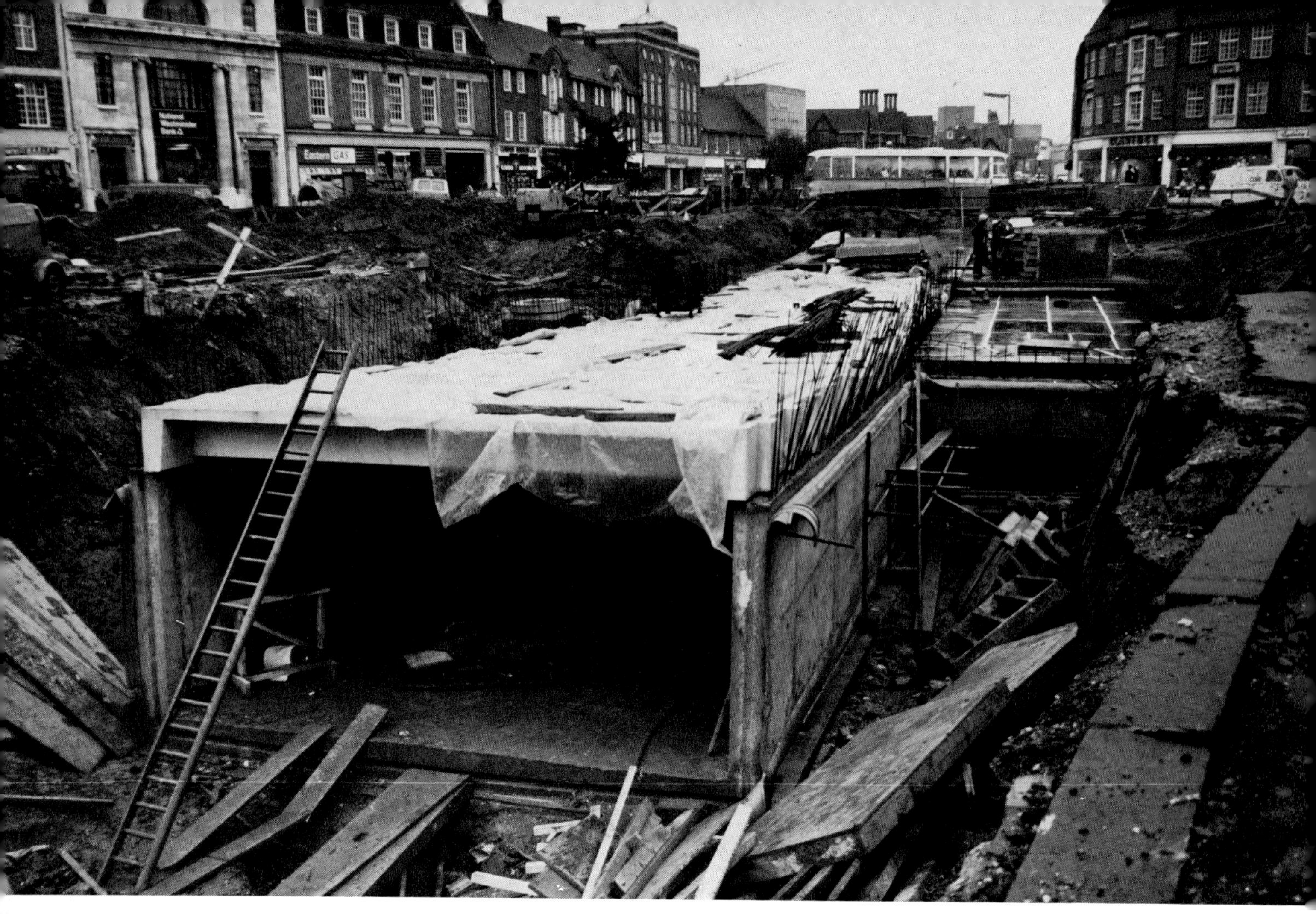
Eastern GAS

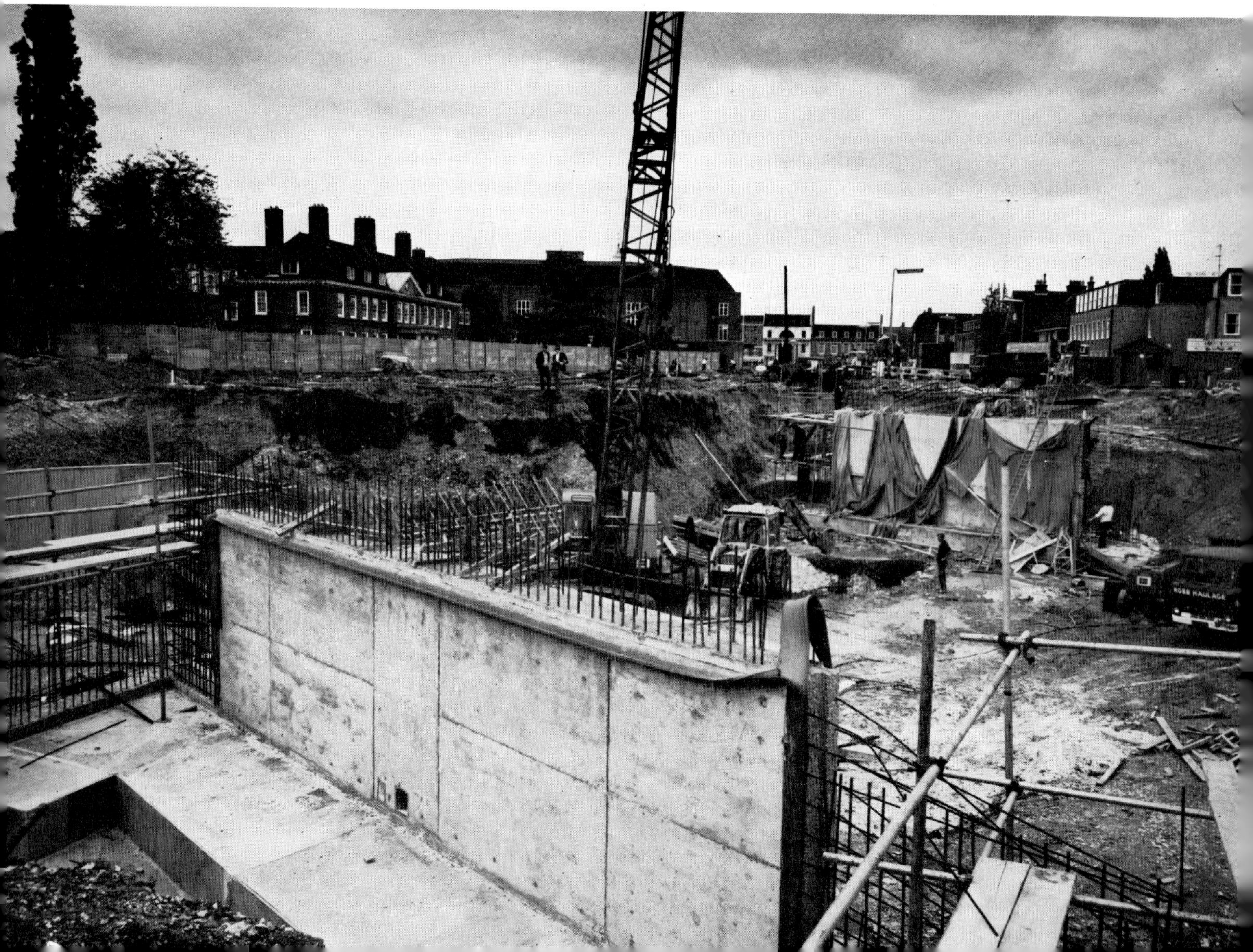

Left: Work being carried out on the pedestrian subway that links the Town Hall and Central Library with the High Street on 1st February, 1972

Below left: Looking towards the Peace Memorial Wing of the Watford General Hospital on 4th August, 1971. In the foreground the bridge near Cassio Road is in an early stage of construction

Above top: The bridge near Cassio Road showing final preparations before concreting on 1st December, 1971

Above: The bridge near Cassio Road giving a view of soffit and columns on 11th January, 1972

St. Mary's Church ▶

St. Mary's is the town's mother church. It is a thirteenth century building, which was extensively restored in 1848 and 1871, and has seen the original village of Watford grow into a sleepy country market town and then become the present thriving commercial and industrial centre. Only a minute or two from the bustling High Street and Corporation Market, St. Mary's and its churchyard form a quiet oasis at the very heart of Watford, and it is here that people can pause for inspiration and comfort, as previous generations have also done for centuries past.

Multi-storey Car Parks

Of all the structures that have appeared in the period after the Second World War, perhaps the most intriguing are multi-storey car parks. These can, of course, be merely brutal and ugly, but in Watford, the Borough Council was determined that structures of this kind would be decorative as well as utilitarian. The result has been the Shrubbery, Church Street and Sutton Road multi-storey car parks, which achieve a grace and elegance often lacking in other buildings. This is especially true at night when alternating bands of light and darkness make them appear to float serenely above their surroundings.

Above: Church Street multi-storey car park. Constructed by Holst & Co Ltd

Below: Sutton Road multi-storey car park. Constructed by Holst & Co Ltd

The breezy call of incense-breathing Morn,
The swallow twitt'ring from the straw-built shed,
The cock's shrill clarion, or the echoing horn,
No more shall rouse them from their lowly bed.

For them no more the blazing hearth shall burn,
Or busy housewife ply her evening care:
No children run to lisp their sire's return,
Or climb his knees the envied kiss to share.

Thomas Gray
Elegy written in a Country Churchyard

Acknowledgements

It would be impossible to produce a work of this kind without the help of a large number of people. I would therefore like to thank in particular Alderman Hubert Buckingham, who is playing such a prominent part in this year's Jubilee celebrations, Mr. Harry Horwood, Mr. Albert Dillingham and Mr. Leonard Johnson. They have all lightened my task considerably by identification of material from the earlier part of the century and have given me the benefit of their wisdom acquired collectively in service on the Borough Council, which, if added together, comes to more than one hundred years.

Also, I owe a great debt to Mr. Gordon Hall, the Town Clerk, and his staff, especially Mr. Philip Judge and Miss Muriel Wood. In addition I have received much valuable advice from Mr. Richard Brand, the Borough Engineer and Surveyor, and his staff, and especially Mr. Brian Williams, the Special Projects Engineer for Phase 3 of the Central Area Redevelopment Scheme. Finally, it gives me particular pleasure in acknowledging the work of Miss Margaret Marshall, the Borough Reference Librarian, of my own staff. She has not only made many suggestions for the improvement of this Pictorial History, but has also carried out the onerous task of reading proofs and checking all the layouts.

Photographic Sources

Watford Public Libraries own an extensive photographic collection of the town and this is in large measure due to the vision and energy of George Bolton, the Borough Librarian from 1919 to 1950. As well as being qualified in his own chosen profession, he was also a keen photographer and an A.R.P.S. Unfortunately, very few of the photographs used in this work can be definitely attributed to him, although it seems clear that he was responsible at least for the fine series on flooding in the Lower High Street and those covering the General Strike and the Second World War. The one photograph that actually bears his name is of a ward in the Peace Memorial Hospital, and I purposely prevented it from being erased, when the block was being prepared, as a small and inadequate tribute to his skill.

William Bickerton, who was Mayor in 1931/32, and led the campaign to save the Bedford Almshouses from demolition, was a brilliant photographer and an F.R.P.S. He was especially gifted in taking birds, but fortunately for posterity also used his camera to give us many of the pictures that I have used in the sequence on Cassiobury. Both the frontispiece and the aerial view of Cassiobury House were produced by the Central Aerophoto Co. Ltd.

Members of the Watford Camera Club have placed at my disposal the special work produced for their 1972 Jubilee Year Exhibition, which covers various aspects of life in the town, and my grateful thanks go to Frank Weemys A.R.P.S. for his sequence on the Market (pp71 and 72), Ronald Smithers A.R.P.S. for his shots of the Watford Football Club (p53), Derek Andrews for the panoramic view of Watford Junction (p45), Edward Burgis for the 727 express coach (p47), Barry Anthony for the crane driver and lighting columns in the section on the Central Area Redevelopment (p75) and Frederick Mayer for his evocative study of St. Mary's Church that ends this work (p79).

After the Second World War sequence, attribution becomes relatively easy and I would like to acknowledge the work of the following individuals, institutions, newspapers and agencies:

Peter Coppock p66 Student doing film make-up for printing
Stuart Kinch p24 The Grove
Malcolm Orvis p49 Modern 142 bus p56 Ski-slope p65 College of Technology p66 Boys' Grammar School p67 Exterior and interior of Cassiobury Junior School p68 Hollytree House p69 Caractacus Green p70 High Street Precinct and View towards Boots
Bill Beck p74 Odhams Printing Works
Graphic Photos Ltd. p12 The Mace p26 Exterior of Bedford Almshouses p49 No. 142 bus in 1920s p55 Cyclocross pp62 & 63 H.R.H. the Queen Mother p69 Exterior and interior view of Harebreaks estate house
Theodore Greville Studios pp22 & 23 Lodge Gates, crests and dated brick p28 Exterior of new Maternity Unit p29 Interior of new Maternity Unit p37 Interior of Palace Theatre and scene from a production p39 Firemen in gasmasks p51 Bridge over Grand Union Canal p52 Grand Union Canal p54 Hempstead Road Baths p57 Exterior of Central Library p67 Interior of Meriden Infants' School p68 View of houses in the Cassiobury estate
Gregg Couper & Co. p65 Exterior of Cassio College
C. F. W. Holmes pp76 & 77 Four views of Central Area Redevelopment
Victoria & Albert Museum p17 Roundel
British Transport Commission p46 Signal box and train used on half-hourly fast service to Euston p47 Royal Scot
London Transport p48 Train leaving Moor Park
Cape Universal Building Products Ltd. p73 Cape Universal Offices
H. J. Heinz & Co. Ltd. p73 Heinz Offices
S. Hille & Co. Ltd. & Erno Goldfinger p73 S. Hille & Co. Premises
Holst & Co. Ltd. p78 Church Street and Sutton Road Multi-storey Car Parks
West Herts Post p28 Exterior of Peace Memorial Hospital p58 Presentation at Odhams and Young Visitors p61 Waiting crowd and H.R.H. the Duke of Edinburgh with children
Echo & Post p51 Falling leaves and children in Cassiobury Park p55 Tennis instruction p59 The Mayor and visitors from Nanterre p65 H.R.H. the Duchess of Kent
Aerofilms & Aero Pictorial Ltd. p54 Woodside Arena
Three Star Press Agency p59 House of Commons visit
Keystone Press Agency Ltd. p44 Harrow & Wealdstone train crash
Scammell Lorries Ltd. p74 Tanker Lorry
Sun Printers Ltd. p74 Section of main Press Room

Inevitably, even after a great deal of patient research, there are photographs the ownership of which I cannot identify. I can only apologise to the photographers concerned and hope that the inclusion of their work is some recompense for its lack of attribution.